FARM ANIMALS

Goats

Jared Siemens

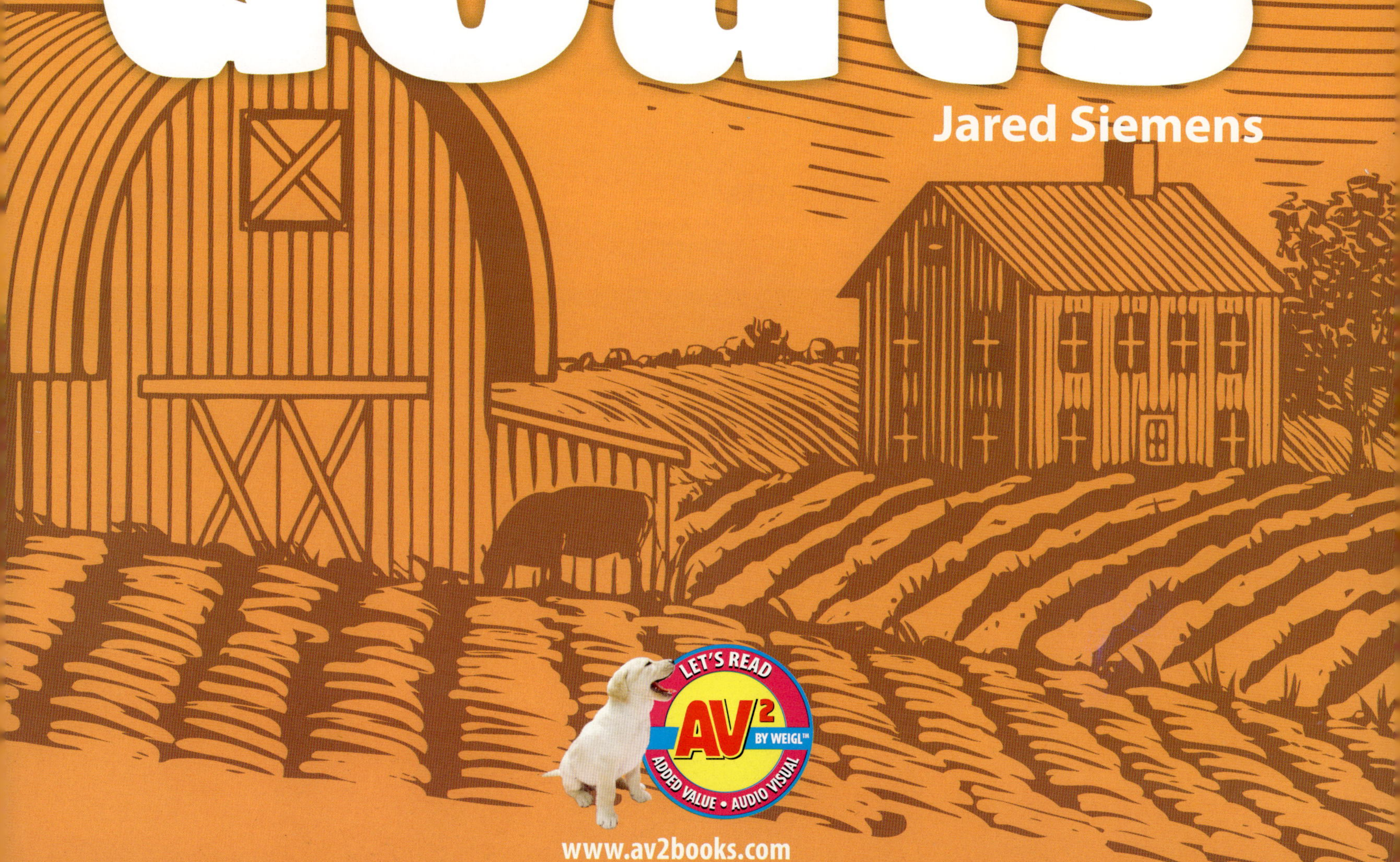

LET'S READ AV² BY WEIGL™ ADDED VALUE • AUDIO VISUAL

www.av2books.com

Go to www.av2books.com, and enter this book's unique code.

BOOK CODE

AVY66849

AV² by Weigl brings you media enhanced books that support active learning.

AV² provides enriched content that supplements and complements this book. Weigl's AV² books strive to create inspired learning and engage young minds in a total learning experience.

Your AV² Media Enhanced books come alive with...

Audio
Listen to sections of the book read aloud.

Video
Watch informative video clips.

Embedded Weblinks
Gain additional information for research.

Try This!
Complete activities and hands-on experiments.

Key Words
Study vocabulary, and complete a matching word activity.

Quizzes
Test your knowledge.

Slide Show
View images and captions, and prepare a presentation.

... and much, much more!

Published by AV² by Weigl
350 5th Avenue, 59th Floor New York, NY 10118
Website: www.av2books.com

Library of Congress Cataloging-in-Publication Data

Names: Siemens, Jared, author.
Title: Goats / Jared Siemens.
Description: New York, NY : Published by AV² by Weigl, 2018. | Series: Farm animals | Includes index.
Identifiers: LCCN 2018050065 (print) | LCCN 2018051559 (ebook) | ISBN 9781489695420 (Multi User Ebook) | ISBN 9781489695437 (Single User Ebook) | ISBN 9781489695406 (hardcover : alk. paper) | ISBN 9781489695413 (softcover : alk. paper)
Subjects: LCSH: Goats--Juvenile literature.
Classification: LCC SF383.35 (ebook) | LCC SF383.35 .S54 2018 (print) | DDC 636.3/9--dc23
LC record available at https://lccn.loc.gov/2018050065

Printed in Guangzhou, China
1 2 3 4 5 6 7 8 9 0 22 21 20 19 18

122018
102918

Art Director: Terry Paulhus Project Coordinator: Jared Siemens

Weigl acknowledges Getty Images, Newscom, Shutterstock, Alamy, and iStock as the primary image suppliers for this title.

FARM ANIMALS

Goats

In this book you will learn

- how they look
- what they do
- what they eat
- why we keep them
- and much more!

G

A goat is an animal that lives on a farm.

oats

Farmers keep goats for their milk and wool.

There are nearly 1,000,000 goats in Texas.

A baby goat is called a kid.

Most kids are born in the spring.

Goats have four strong legs.

A goat has a hoof on the end of each leg.

Goat hoofs have two toes.

A goat grows horns on its head.

Both male and female goats can grow horns.

Goat horns never stop growing.

Goats talk to each other with a "baaa" sound.

This is called **bleating.**

Goats eat shrubs and weeds.

They spend most of their days eating.

Goats chew their food **two** times.

Goats are excellent climbers. Some goats will climb trees to eat berries.

Goats are very social.

They like to live together in large groups.

Goats need plenty of open space to feed and roam.

Open spaces help goats stay healthy.

GOAT FACTS

These pages provide detailed information that expands on the interesting facts found in the book. They are intended to be used by adults as a learning support to help young readers round out their knowledge of each unique animal featured in the *Farm Animals* series and why it is kept and raised on farms.

Pages 4–5

A goat is an animal that lives on a farm. Wisconsin produces more goat's milk than any other state. Globally, more people consume goat's milk than milk from any other animal. Goats are also kept for their hair. Goat hair is often woven into soft fabrics and used to make blankets, or spun into yarn and used to make sweaters.

Pages 6–7

A baby goat is called a kid. Pregnant female goats carry their kids for about five months before giving birth. When she gives birth, it is called "kidding." A female goat can have a litter of up to six kids at once, though twins and triplets are much more common. Each kid has a unique scent, which helps its mother recognize it.

Pages 8–9

Goats have four strong legs. Each of a goat's four legs ends in a cloven, or two-toed, hoof. Due to the shape of the hoof, its soft sole, and the splay of its toes, goats have traction in almost every kind of terrain. Adult domestic goats usually weigh about 100 pounds (45 kilograms), while some breeds can reach adult weights of up to 250 pounds (113 kg).

Pages 10–11

A goat grows horns on its head. A goat's horns are hollow, and may be curved or curled like a corkscrew. Goats use their horns to protect themselves from predators. Male goats typically have larger horns than female goats. An American-owned goat named Uncle Sam once held the world record for longest horn spread, at 52 inches (132 centimeters) wide. In 2017, an Austrian-owned goat named Rasputin took the record. His horns measure 53.23 inches (135.2 cm) from tip to tip.

Pages 12–13

Goats talk to each other with a "baaa" sound. For the most part, goats are relatively quiet animals. When a goat bleats, it may be asking for attention or expressing stress. Each goat has a unique bleat. This helps a mother goat to identify which of her kids is calling to her.

Pages 14–15

Goats eat shrubs and weeds. Goats are ruminants, which means they are herbivores with four-chambered stomachs. In order to digest food completely, goats have to chew and swallow their food once, spit it up, and chew it a second time. This complex digestive process allows goats to eat quickly and store large amounts of roughage, such as grass and hay, to digest later.

Pages 16–17

Goats are excellent climbers. Having developed to survive steep, mountainous terrain, goats are incredibly agile. Some breeds have been known to climb steep cliffs, dams, and even trees. Goats have a natural inclination to forage and will often stand on their hind legs to reach food in low-lying tree branches.

Pages 18–19

Goats are very social. Goats are friendly animals that prefer to live in the company of other goats. They often live in groups called herds. Goat herds are typically led by one male goat, or billy, and one female goat, or doe. The average herd size on farms in the United States is about 30 goats.

Pages 20–21

Goats need plenty of open space to feed and roam. Goats are instinctive browsers, and are happiest when they can roam open fields freely. Farmers should place gate latches out of a goat's reach when building a fence or an enclosure where their goats will be kept. Goats are very intelligent, and can learn how to open these latches.

KEY WORDS

Research has shown that as much as 65 percent of all written material published in English is made up of 300 words. These 300 words cannot be taught using pictures or learned by sounding them out. They must be recognized by sight. This book contains 54 common sight words to help young readers improve their reading fluency and comprehension. This book also teaches young readers several important content words, such as proper nouns. These words are paired with pictures to aid in learning and improve understanding.

Page	Sight Words First Appearance
4	a, an, animal, farm, is, lives, on, that
5	and, are, for, in, keep, their, there
7	most, the
8	four, have
9	each, end, has, of, two
10	both, can, grows, head, its, never, stop
12	another, one, sound, talk, this, to, with
15	days, eat, food, they, times
16	some, trees, will
19	groups, large, like, together, very
20	need, open
21	help

Page	Content Words First Appearance
4	goat
5	farmers, milk, Texas, wool
7	baby, kid, spring
8	legs
9	hoof, toes
10	horns
12	bleating
15	shrubs, weeds
16	berries, climbers
20	space